The Springtime of Lovers   *Rumi*

The springtime of Lovers has come,
That this dust bowl may become a Paradise;
The proclamation of heaven has come,
That the bird of the soul may rise in flight;
The sea becomes full of pearls,
The salt marsh becomes as sweet as Kauthar;
The stone becomes a ruby from the mine,
The body becomes utterly soul.

*

SAMA
GHAZAL
SALAAM
UK

Poetry and Lyrics

First published in the United Kingdom by
electraglade/Shutter Books 2009
ISBN 978-0-9551307-7-9

All poetry collected and edited by Chris Firth, with help from Gareth Spark, Deborah Firth and Asif Firfirey.
Cover design – electraglade, with design and production assistance from Creative Studio Design Ltd, Yorkshire.

www.creativestudiodesign.co.uk
Page design and formatting by East Coast Books, Yorkshire
(thanks to Michael Wray).
Cover image and art work is copyrighted by
electraglade/Chris Firth © 2009

Contact, queries and comments: samaghazal@hotmail.co.uk
Facebook: sama ghazal

This publication was enabled through the support and assistance of Arts Council England (non-lottery funding), The UK Muslim Writers' Awards and Electraglade.

ARTS COUNCIL
ENGLAND

SAMA GHAZAL SALAAM UK

Poetry and Lyrics

A collection of Persian, Arabian, Islamic and UK inspired poetry. The contemporary poems here are collected from writers living in the UK. Some of the poems were short-listed entries to the UK Muslim Writers' Awards 2007, 2008 and 2009 (indicated by MWA following the poem).

Collected and edited by Chris Firth
with assistance from Asif Firfirey, Deborah Firth and Gareth Spark.

Thanks for other help and support to Irfan Akram (Innovate Arts Partnerships); Shabana Javid (Muslim Writers' Awards); Sophie Bi (Birmingham Libraries); Afifa Ematullah (text suggestions and glossary); Abdul Wadud/Paul Sutherland (Dream Catcher Magazine); Michael Wray (East Coast Books); Adam Strickson (text suggestions); Lisa White (Middlesbrough Libraries); Richard and Wendy Jemison (Shutter Books); Joe Cooke (cover input); Ahmed Adnan and the Salam-UK Band (support and music) and the Arts Council England.

Contents:

Notes or extra information requested by the writers are indicated by * after the poem. All notes are in the back sections of the book. Thanks to Afifa Ematullah for invaluable assistance and guidance with these notes.

Editor's Introduction

Rumi remarked that 'All talk is a form of boasting'.
In light of his wisdom, this introduction will be short.

Some of the poets published here are Muslims, some are not. Some are previously published poets; some are published here for the first time.

The only requirement for consideration and inclusion in this book was that there had to be some form of inspiration or influence from the Persian poets such as Rumi, Omar, Attar, Saadi and Hafez, or from the Islamic faith and its cultural traditions.
There was no particular well thought out logic or marketing strategy to this; it was just an idea, an inspiration, and perhaps, more importantly, from a feeling of the heart.
Poetry and music will always bring people together, whatever their professed faith, beliefs or chosen religion. This book is evidence of that.

From an editorial point of view, the touch and intervention here has been 'light' – a suggestion here, a tweak there, some tightening of layout and punctuation throughout to meet the demands of limited space. It seemed more important that the voice and expression of the writers emerged rather than every comma and placement of capital letter met the ever shifting universal required standards of English grammatical accuracy.

Despite the book title, 'experts' of the ghazal form will note that, technically speaking, there are few disciplined, form-adhering ghazals in the collection. The good intention (*niyyah*) is there though, so I'm sure that you'll forgive our liberty in using this term in the book's title.

Here is a bridge – please, cross it.
Here is a cup – please, drink deep, then pass it around.

We hope that you will enjoy the many beautiful poems and lyrics we offer to you here.

Evening Song

Chris Firth

The sky is lamp blue,
The horizon black kohl
On the eyelid
Of evening.

The moon is a drum,
The single star cries,
So high, so bright, so pure,
Alone.

Town lights flicker on
Below this hill top;
Thoughts drift through
Long shadows of streets.

Dum dum tak -
The love-drunk moon plays on;
Bubbles hiss
A tambourine of stars;
Slowly
The night comes reeling in.

Join in, join in -
Inevitably
This world
Is in the song.

Thank You, thank You.
Slowly now -
The whole world
Turns into song.

*

The Challenge

Ameena Zameer Hanif

I challenge you
To swim into the perturbed depths
Of the untold heart,
Where that which you do not *see*
Lives in haunting isolation.
I dare you
To dive into the raving nightmares
Of the screaming mind
Where that which you can never *know*
Refuses to be touched by any hand.

Weary Traveller

Ameena Zameer Hanif

Why do you travel in solitude
With no-one to love?
Come rest at my house,
I will provide you with a feast of tenderness.
You have traveled for so long
That you have forgotten what it is like to feel.
Can you not hear the pulse of the earth?
Can you not hear the breathing of the clouds?
Do you not see the red fire of the sun?
Look, oh weary traveller,
You have truly lost the meaning of life.
Why do you travel so -
For whom do you search?

Oceans Of Pearls
Ameena Zameer Hanif

Embedded within the golden pages of The Qur'an
I discovered oceans of pearls
And caskets of untold treasures.
I found an abundance
Of light streaming between surahs,
Ascending through each line
And bursting through every verse.
In troubled times
I saw how Allah's words spoke directly to me
As they eased my mind
Into calmer waves of cooled emotion.
The vast sea of questions, once roaming aimlessly,
Has been resolved by the ease of answers
Rippling from the current of sparas, surahs and ayats.
At night, my soul flew away
Into the temporary domain of dreams
Where I read from the glorious pages of The Holy Qur'an.
I have seen the power of Allah demonstrated
Through reflective parables,
As each one gives a spiritual insight
Into Islam's magnificence.
When I talk to others about Islam
I think about The Words
Floating in the treasury of my memory
And they flow from my lips
Like the pure zamzam water that springs in Mecca.
Ultimately, I find that The Holy Qur'an
Impels me to revise its contents over and over
So that the torch in my mind
Remains brighter with everlasting truths.

Beyond The Veil   *David C. Byrne*

That girl over there with a name somewhere in her tongue,
with skin wrapped all over her, and those sad eyes, jewels;
pools of amber that swim as I drip into them and undo my Christianity.

Her tawny woven scarf sleeps on her, undulates and is secretly caressed,
folded away. I play with icons, sling Jesus around my neck for fashion,
blush at confession, dress myself in blame and guilt but still pray.

What is her hair? Is it a curl and sprinkle, a spiral that sings on a mosque
floor? There are more shapes and I imagine, undo a curve from her,
a lock of something, a rapture that is gone, lost to a storm,

a gust, a hurricane. I see my mother straighten my tie, knot tissue for
clean ears, God sees all men, God sees all boys. Again my hands
close together for prayer, for way back when I did not know my outcome.

That girl over there shies pins into her hair for Allah, clips and tucks,
plucks words from The Qur'an, mumbles something important.
May we be closer to heaven? May we be together where I circle

fingers in rings and loops of hair, see those amber eyes droop
and lift upon me and my Christianity, free from cross and moon and star, where
there are no words for this, where there are no prayers.

That girl over there with a name somewhere in her tongue,
with a skin wrapped all over her, sees me and my Christianity,
my sad eyes, jewels, pools of blue that swim and drip and wait.

In The Dust

Brian D'Arcy

O India, gods and demons scattered in the dust;
their cosmic dance leaves only footprints in the dust.

Once mountains trembled and the holy rivers flowed,
apsaras led the way - light footprints in the dust.

Great battles fought where heroes left their monuments
to stand beside the pilgrims' footprints in the dust.

Your wheel of time still marks the passing of the day,
but human visions blur those footprints in the dust.

The rishis' silent wisdom and the mystic dream:
all now reduced to faded footprints in the dust.

One day you may return to lead me safely home;
or Brian must then follow footprints in the dust.

*

Valentine's Day

Abu Madjnuun

And the city streets are full of smiling lovers
Remembering love, proud that they are true lovers.

Beneath evergreen trees, sheltered from strumming rain,
Through parks they stroll; cheeks graze, arms link; true sworn lovers.

In their eyes burns delightful pleasure in their pain,
Remembering that it must hurt to be lovers.

In bustling afternoon cafes they wine and dine
At special discount prices for embraced lovers,

Or outside hotel doors with no missed calls they pine
Yearning after their unrequiting lovers.

With love sworn by his heart, Madjnuun destroys a rose
As it states that you must not in 'Rules of Lovers'.

A Beautiful Revelation *Nafees Mahmud*

your heart is a blank page
awaiting a love story to be written on it
the bridge of eye contact cannot be walked across
as the toll of your veil is a price too high to pay
for a man already in spiritual bankruptcy

I'll spill an ocean of ink and swim across
keeping my soul afloat with words
in the hope I will arrive at the shore
of your heart

you are faceless to the world
but I see your eyes from afar
the lashes of your angel eyes
whip me into a frenzy and I become
a dervish whirling, a hurricane of
insatiable lust, knowing only love
can cure me but my lust is for love
and my love is for lust

I am the good and the bad
the rational and the base
I am human
and your eyes are the enchanting mirrors
which showed me so

you are as beautiful as the blossom on trees
in early summer, clothing the branches
decorating them in a shyness
as if they dislike exposure
to the world around them

but my all too human heart
loves the season of autumn
will you be like the trees then?
stripped down, naked and bare
revealing all?

life is revelation
the truth is we are human
let my flesh meet yours
let love be written on the blank page
of your heart allowing us to unite as One
like He who created us

Blessed Curse

Abu Madjnuun

Day break again.
I wash my face clean
Of the rubber mask of numbing wine.
I wash my tongue, teeth and breath
Free from the leer of night.
Oh Lord,
In the evenings
A clutch of spiders
Inhabits the caverns of my heart.
Thank God
I'm also blessed with an angel
Who drives them out
With new songs every morning.
I wash my hands clean from the body
And seek to dry them
So that they do not smudge
Or hinder the flow of Your ink
Upon this paper ladder.
I leap up and play the lute
To remind myself of the dumb gift
I am presented with.
I listen to the birds in my own garden
To know the futility of my monkey hand
Upon the strings.
Oh Lord,
In the evenings
Such an animal does laugh and drool in me.
Thank God
I'm also blessed by angels
Who chain him
And dance him around the floorboards
Like the greatest dervish puppet
This mad house has ever seen.

Arrhythmia

Shameam Akhtar MWA

A city on the banks of a river
marches to many rhythms.

An effluence of bad questions and
impossible answers flow through it.

At times, ruled by caprice,
it skips between two meanings -
the dark forest momentarily loses
its trail of bloody footprints
down to where they resume again
by the water's edge.

Then something unexplained -
a fluttering
high in the canopy,
a disturbance,
not fight
but the halt and turn
of the primordial memory
that ignites
the eternal heart;

a bird
startled to flight.

How To Create A Whirlpool   *Shameam Akhtar*

Start with a precise calculation of the cosmos
or recover a particular moment in your space -
the height of a tree,
the length of this room,
the distance from London to Sydney.
Take the basic tenets of
'hello' and 'goodbye'
and attach them to an idea.
Tuck the motive securely inside
the original space.
Disguise it with a song or a dance.
You choose.
Fashion the soul from a design
that insists on fate
and the law of averages,
though secretly you don't believe in either.
Its motif will be you and me
or any urban myth grounded in the science
of whirlpools.
Assume the veneer of loss.
Walk round the outside.
Smile.
Eventually,
disappear.

Paper Thin   *Shameam Akhtar*

There is a moment when
the sky
in the grief of surrender
throws a veil across the
receding light and under cover
of heaven's stolen constellation,
the sorcerer's hand lifts the sea,
shaking it like a sheet.

Displaced by the geometry of
reason,
seagulls patrol the city skyline.

In the distance, a train pulls away
from the station,
windows blacked out.
A man reclines into himself.
I cannot read if,
familiar with the deceits of his age,
he settles into the frame or
if the twitch of his lower lip
signals defeat.
The train rattles on its course,
carriages tethered precariously
to their rickety conversation
in cold steel
of first instinct
and voodoo enlightenment.
Death keeps an ear to the ground
and expectation is the shadow
of a bird passing overhead.
But still they come,
paper Kings and Queens:
Cross my heart
Hope to die.

A Large Qur'an

Adam Strickson

*(similar to work done at
Shiraz, Iran, in the 1370s)*

We stand among the lustre of tiles,
adjust to the dim, cloister light
as if waiting for the stretch of bats
behind glass in the nocturnal house.

I ask my friends, some in jackets,
some in kurtas, all hushed by ornament,
to name their most beautiful,
their Sesame of gold, crystal, silk.

I ask, though I know the answer.
One stall in this priceless bazaar draws all:
a cursive monument of ink and gilt
whose frozen rhythm demands breath.

This crack of lightning shook Arabia.
It's *'Doctor Everything, voyage, mooring,
the bride behind the veil, the deepest well'*,
the beginning and the endless.

My friends were once half faithful boys
who struggled with the dots and swirls
of compassionate and merciful syllables
as the mullah droned out the summer.

Now, their cock crow is grandchildren.
They know The Qur'an cleans hearts,
dips starlings in iridescent glaze,
reveals the star maps of faith.

In Gladstone Street, Rhodes Street,
five times a day they pray, wake
the desert sounds, illuminate
the hour, find light in their mouths.

*

The Minbar of Sultan Qa'itbay

Adam Strickson
(made in the period 1468 – 96)

Spangled with stars, as high as an oak tree,
inlaid with elephants' tusk, this radiant pulpit
preaches geometry, how everything intersects
in the mightiness of the Word, how the foci
of converging lines, the evenness of spaces
show a gifted promise, a yesness of meaning.

Imagine it beyond the slats of the city souk
in downtown Cairo, where the squelched
pink of over-ripe guavas stenches September
and sheep stew in fiery cauldrons big as rooms.

Wash up, enter, bow down, pray, leave pride
and meat smoke at the door, face the mihrab;
watch the imam approach the minbar's arch.
He opens two leaves, climbs heavenwards,
inhabits the heart-wood of the one craftsman
who hid his hand in exactness of repetition.

In mill town mosques with window bars,
bass boom and punches are left outside.
Two stone steps suggest such a minbar:
men bow down, praise God's geometry.

*

8.30 am - most days *Adam Strickson*

In People's Park we walk and breathe, kamiz concealed
in anoraks to trounce the rain, earth under us.

And as we walk we climb again, hike mountain tracks
that browed our childhood years with snow, earth under us.

We walk around the broken glass, swish past the war,
conceive the English love for lines, earth under us.

Our stiff mill knees begin to ease, and yet we grieve
when weeds in chimneys catch the breeze, earth under us.

A circuit walked, we start again, move up a gear
to cheek this morning's sullen wheeze, earth under us.

Hydrangeas blue and pink our walk, explode the wash
and wet of green we've learnt to breathe, earth under us.

We walk among ourselves in hush, and long for heat
to dry this plush of blooms and leaves, earth under us.

O let us walk and breathe, breathe and walk, earth under us,
before Allah rolls up our rugs of time, earth over us,
earth under us, earth under us, earth over us.

Radiotherapy *Dr Debjani Chatterjee, MBE*

Even in these wolf-sharp days your beauty fells me,
Surya; it sears like saffron lava on my chest.

Steer your sky-chariot, wild cloud-horses rampant,
Straining the years like saffron lava on my chest.

Golden god, I would feel your fiery fingertips,
Though they thrust spears like saffron lava on my chest.

My eyes plead for your passionate arms to lift me -
Your clasp that cheers like saffron lava on my chest.

My heart aches to salute but my arms disobey,
So take these tears like saffron lava on my chest.

Surya, let your balmy healer's face shine on me
And melt my fears like saffron lava on my chest.

*

Bedtime Story

'Tis the season when guardians
become lovers and lovers
become gate-keepers
having loved you for eons enough

in the summer there is no heat
anymore just visions of apocalypse
my assumption to become one
with the sky of the mind

wary of stars traversing distances
vast in sleep I watch
blackbirds peering through clouds
wanting to come back down

perhaps too late
for dogs have sprouted wings
cats have climbed and climbed
their way back up from this ground

in their holy houses
fervent Catholics pray for our condition
Muslims avidly count the Signs
one by one whispering
as men with long hair and women with heads
shaved walk by complaining about the weather

It's a Sign
I was told in a present life.

A past to which I never went back.
I was doomed.
I had shaved my head.

*

Shadows and Dust   *Ahmed Khan*

I wear this fraudulent mask with guile;
My hypocrisy roams freely, shackled by none.
Falsehood runs deep in my blood,
Wrapping tightly around my veins,
Soaking me through,
Every glance an inspiration for lies and deceit,
My beating breath a tsunami lie;
In my utterances seas are poisoned.
Abandon me, world, I am a worthless wretch.
Leave me to die in the desert sands,
Parched lips cracked, with thorns as fodder.
I have opened my chest a thousand times;
Its reflection sees only idols, false gods and snakes.
Did you really think you could fly on sweet scented musk?
After traversing the earth why do you aspire for rum?
What have you memorized with your tongue?
Do you dare to sip from the cup?
Layla, romance me no more
For this heart was never a rose garden.
Awake me no more, let me sleep forever.
I swear, in this heart there is no good.
In my death, place no headstone for rest;
I pray my existence be a memory vanished.
Waste not your tears with my lament
For my life was worthlessly spent.
Sever me quick, for every breath is a false life.
Ishtiyaaq, you have uttered your beings,
Say it for the last time.

*

Jealous Ensemble   *Ahmed Khan*

Crickets rub their hind legs;
An ensemble begins.
Bells ring out.
Clapping with rosewood batons,
I call you out to dance.
Inject me with your mosquito love!
What do I need to do to prove I am yours?
Lovelorn, do not be jealous,
You know I only twirl this baton with you.
Clapping hands, me and you,
Flesh sliding on skin,
We are union, we are one;
Colleagues and friends are all stars twinkling
In and out of time.
You are my moon, constant;
What do I need to do to prove I am yours?
Arched back chiming to your pain,
Yoga manoeuvres say yes,
Sliding my hand in parched air;
My movement has its own wish,
Its own expression.
Lovelorn, do not be jealous.

Spiritual Ecstasy   *Sufi Punk*

As the music fuses
Strings from the guitar
Flirt with the tabla beat
My heart becomes the dance floor
Overwhelmed with every beat
My heart's seduced by the sounds
I want to become the music
I hear you play in the round
Heightened excitement is the energy
That is lifting spirits for everybody
Leaving them smiling
My temperature has begun rising
And as I feel moved, my eyes begin to fill with pearls
Joy and happiness sprinkle over us like shining rainfall
The clapping and chanting
Is like a night breeze
Bringing with it answers and setting my worries at ease
The music a gold silk cloth
That wraps itself around the audience, joining us in
Our movement and our song
I see the purpose of creation
Acted out before my eyes
All paths leading to one destination
That includes all walks of life
Each with its own blueprint
But connected at that point in time
We became this rave of devotion
Full of love and feeling alive
The guitar collects the heart strings
From whoever submits
I recognise the music of souls
Our aura whirls in circles in memory of our beloved
I've turned into the melody
And flow charmingly from your lips
Lost momentarily in eternal bliss
I become your recollection
Words by which you are remembered
I'm music to which we sing
'Mauallah ya Salli wasallum da iman abadun...'

The Music   *Ustaz Fitrah*

Thank God
For the music,
Allah Kareem
For the music,
The tune has chewed me up,
The tune has spat me out
And replaced me with myself.

I am not
In the music,
I am not
In the music,
The tune has ground me down,
The tune has gouged me out
And replaced me with itself.

I am destroyed
By the music,
I am destroyed
By the music,
The tune has burnt me up,
The tune has put me out
And replaced me with nothing else.

My life is
The music,
My life is
The music,
The tune has thrown me out,
The tune has thrown me through the door
Replacing me with silent space.

Thank God
For the music
Alhumdilillah
For the music,
The tune that takes a man of clay
And leaves in place
a bird in flight.

Nightfall Song

Ustaz Fitrah

Night falls, night falls,
But you are still away, my love,
Night falls, nights falls,
So far, far away
From this old town.

Full moon, full moon
But you are still away, my love,
Night falls, night falls,
So far, far away
Past the mountain.

Bright stars, bright stars
But you are still away, my love,
Night falls, night falls
So far, far away
Over the water.

Wind howls, wind howls,
But you are still away, my love,
Night falls, night falls,
So far, far away
From these knots of my heart.

The white frost of dawn
Threads the horizon.
Sunlight has kissed
The feet of the mountain.
Light dances
Upon the river and ocean.
Surely, one day soon,
You will be coming home, my love?
Then, and only then
Will I be glad
To see night fall.

Landscape

Mariette Thorburn

This is
a strange country:
wafered leaves
sucked of colour,
grey mist,
flattened hills
and life
suspended.

I will be here
for a while
lost and wandering
through
this landscape
of bones
and broken speeches,
untangling the words
you left
trapped like fleece
on ling flowers.

Here
the night speaks
in monotones
and no one
can find me.
Only you
are the one
who can
guide me through
this limbo
back to the
warm, moonlit
belly of the valley
where windows glow,
where hearts beat loud
and sing from
all the houses.

Kissing The Ground

Nooruddean Choudry MWA

Kissing the ground
Is not beneath me
I close my eyes
And it elevates me
This blessed space
A magic carpet
My senses soar
Forehead on floor.
Kissing the ground
I reach beyond me
I feel Him near
And it elevates me
I leave this place
And find my peace
On my journey
Lost in hymn.
Kissing the ground
Seeking mercy
I pray in verse
And it elevates me
This time is mine
And His alone
My paradise found
Kissing the ground.

Sleepless In Recital

Nooruddean Choudry MWA

The silence of the night crumbles at my lips.
I'm sleepless in recital of flawless pearls
Passed on to me like blessed ornaments,
Gifted from another world, fashioned of the
Soulful night song of some distant paradise.
In the stillness of this place I whisper alone
And yet the voices of countless others join me,
Echoing the same soul music in flawless chorus,
Verse upon verse upon verse on forever.
These words will not sparkle and die over time
For this everlasting constellation only grows,
Piercing the darkness and lighting the way.

Ego Unwound

Asif Firfirey

Sunset Maghrib,
the world in hushed tones.
Curtains were drawn
while we climbed steps
to a shrine on the slopes
to wash in a stream
and pray,
the words of our impromptu imam
cushioned by layers
of green and red satin.
Later that night
back on the beach
something happened
watched by 12 stone Apostles
and perhaps something more
without words
without warning
all of us
just
let
Go
no music
apart from the wind
whispering 'Allah'
and waves kissing sand
like lips mouthing 'Muhammad'
and we whirled
not knowing what to call it
our hands and feet
moving us
and we followed
ego unwound.
That night
four came undone
and witnessed
the One.

*

Eid Mubarak

Asif Firfirey

He'd come into my room early,
hairy pot-belly straining against
a towel too small,
face flecked with foam.
'It's time,' he'd say.

Little Cotton-wool balls
dipped in Jannatul Firdous
or some other concentrated sweetness
from a cigar box filled with Alchemist's delights:
no Cohibar or Monte Cristo
but attar with ambergris, or musk or rose
and placed just so
in just the right bit of my ear,
the remnants on oily fingers
rubbed on my new clothes
but lightly so they didn't stain.

When I was too tall
for a comfortable embrace
he stood on the raised pavement
outside
or the second step
inside,
his fuzzy cheek to mine smooth,
his moustache tickling
'Eid Mubarak' in my ear.

*

I Miss My Father's Embrace

Romana Qureshi MWA

A humble man sits before us,
His light, wit and smiles inspire us,
He tells us of the true message,
With beauty, conviction and silence,
We in awe - his wisdom, Your guidance,
He shares a story,
Of the loss of his father,
Emotions change. We feel his pain.
We see it in his face.
He misses his father's embrace.

A beautiful woman sits before us,
The *noor* in her eyes,
Captivating realness.
With *saffa* she tells us of the conviction in her heart,
How she travelled to His House,
Cried, O Allah, let us never be apart,
Of her father protecting her,
In a white sea of crowds,
Kissing her forehead,
Daughter, I will forever be proud,
We see tears roll down her face;
At that very moment
She misses her father's embrace.

A part of who I am stands before me,
He places his hand softly on my head,
Gives a thousand blessings for the journey ahead,
I hover around him as he leaves for *Jummah*,
He stops, turns and smiles,
With affection in his face,
He picks me up - an embrace,
I wonder in that moment how long I will be held,
Wrapped in happiness, I surrender, I drown,
Knowing I will always miss the beauty of this embrace.
Praying I feel its warmth each and every day,
Remembering the love I see in his face.
I miss my father's embrace.

Mother and Daughter   *Sitara Khan*

Enveloped in thick blanket of dark hair,
scalp stinging, tears rolling,
clamped by her feet,
between my mother's legs, I'd sit.

Tugging, pulling,
her dainty oiled hands
combed and disentangled their way
through my unruly mass;
Ritualistic taming symbolized in the plaits.

Weighed by tradition I struggled to be free,
daring to dream of bob cuts
and hair dressers' salons.
School mates' envy brought little relief.

My mother's instinct whispered in my ear:
'Mother's loving milk has nurtured your hair.
In its lustrous length is woven the yarn
from ancestral antiquity to who I am now.
With this dowry I do thee trust,
which for other cares you must not neglect.'

The bonding tie between mother and daughter such
That scissors of rebellion could not quite touch.

Rocking The Cradle　　　Sitara Khan

Baghdad, the first born, hand
that rocked the cradle of civilisation.
With Tigris and Euphrates in her veins,
she held tight the fount,
drew in majestic sovereigns and beggars of pearls,
 who pushed Zero to infinity.

The Hanging Gardens of flowers,
fruits and palms ring in the
oceanic consciousness: jasmine junnah
in the Zanana.

Quail lulled the bounteous Babu
and the lark sang daily reveille.
Date stones fuelled the earthen oven,
fluttering flaming lashes at the onion bread.

Cedar packed camel caravans,
traced through glistening sand to the Pharaonic Nile.
Persian stallions glided to Ethiopia
with silver chandeliers for the emperor.
China's worms threaded the road with silk,
porcelain urns, in oriental bazaars
spun yarns of Scheherazade.

For one thousand and one nights,
her death knocked, closet locked,
the King captured. Leila, in the star lit
Arabian night, rubbed the enchanted lamp.

*

*This is the opening extract of a longer poem by Sitara,
exploring aspects of the evolution of civilization.*

A Letter To The Prophet   *Aysha Khanom*

'We have sent you (O Muhammad) as a mercy for all the nations.'
(al-Qur'an 21:107)
If I saw your smile, I would cry out of happiness,
If I saw your tears, I would cry out of sadness.
If only I could have been there to catch your tears;
I look into the mirror and wish to see you there.
When times are hard I wish for your company;
Your smile alone would dispel my sorrows.
When times are hard,
I ask myself, what would you advise me?
I first read about you, and your mercy and compassion towards others,
and I fell in love.
I pray to Allah to help me follow your footsteps,
Just to even sit where you sat,
Walk where you walked.
You are my role model,
My reflection in the mirror which I can't yet see.
I want to love what you love, and dislike that which you dislike.
I stand in prayer and look to my side, wishing you were there.
You are the friend I am searching for
But I know I will never find;
You truly are the 'one' out of mankind.
If I was ever given the chance to catch a glimpse of you
I would travel from the West to the East.
I only wish to be like you,
I miss you...
I can now only wish to be the closest to you on the Day of Qiyamah,
because even then I will be comforted by your presence.
I thank Allah for making me part of your Ummah,
and it is above an honour to aspire to be like you.
You truly are a Mercy to Mankind.

Dhikr, Dhikr, Calling, Dhikr

Shelina Zahra Janmohamed

His names are calling me, calling me
I turn and He's there, calling me

Singing in my head, singing to me
I sleep and He's there, singing to me

The trees whisper to me, secretly calling
Calling His name to me, secretly calling

The flowers smile at me, shyly smiling His name
I glance at them, smiling His name

There is no escape from the whisper of His name
The skies and seas whisper His name

Wherever I run, His names are calling
In the rain and the sands, His names are calling

Hiding in the darkness they find me, seeking me out
The mountains and clouds send His names, seeking me
out

I close my eyes and He is there, calling me
His Names sing out, calling me

*

Imaginary Autumn *Shelina Zahra Janmohamed*

When the red blurs into the gold
She steps into the imaginary garden;
She sees his face in the burnished copper leaves,
Reflections of his gentle hand sweeping across her cheek.
Are they real, she wonders, the leaves?

When her body disintegrates will they still be there,
Aflame and crisp, strung between life and death?
The burning trees shoot up into the luminous sky
Where she sees his face
Where she sees his face not.

The dazzling leaves rustle in her heart.
She stretches her hand to touch them;
The white light dissolves it.
The sudden brightness of the sky subsumes her,
A small dot in an imaginary garden.

She turns frantically to the leaves.
Her beloved is no longer there,
Nor in the moss beneath her soles;
Hands no longer light on light,
The tree trunks an image once forgotten.

She spins unbalanced,
Drunk with colour,
Drunk with light.
Where is her beloved?
Where is he not?

The rustling grows louder, deafening inside,
Russet, ochre, bronze and gold,
Around her a tornado of angelic white.
Her flames spill into the blanched autumn paradise,
A fiery dot magnificent in light.

What choice the leaves of life or death?
To float or breathe for beauty's sake,
To turn away the beloved's smile
For a moment's beauty in an imaginary garden.

The Visitor

Paul Sutherland

At his impulsive arrival,
hunting for the lit path

to a Sufi master's house,

he stooped under curves
of an unopened jasmine.
A wadi sounded, running
to a calm roar, in its valley
mountain water searched
for its ocean and diverted
fed cloud-shaped orchards.
Sweet fragrance, held him.
A hung moon altered steps
into apparitions on stone.
He rounded a bend to see
an old wall straying under
a lean-to roof; hurt, plaster
steps crept up to a wicker-
railed porch. Half turning
he panned shadowless sky.
Assembled white iris, under
a date palm's serrated fonts,
spoke galaxies. A worn lamp
blued a breach in a doorway.
His greeting *As salaam alaikum*
carried away in midnight air
the visitor was called inside.

*

The Mosque of Seven Companions

Paul Sutherland

Inside Hazrat Omar Mosque, you -
twenty-five years a covered Muslim
and I - five days from my Shahada -
submit before the tall green alcove
its unfigured hollow topped with
calligraphy you wish you could read.

The Mediterranean's cadences
sound through beats of thought.
Breakers could snarl and hurl
storm-froth on the shelter's roof
yet no weather-mood can perturb
seven green turbaned saints inside.

When, from eight centuries of warring
empires, Ottoman foot soldiers ducked
into a cave and chanced on, laid-out,
unaged bodies of seven companions
they appeared no more than children
cuddling for warmth, ready to awake.

The mosque's far-eyed attendant
collects for the abstract-bordered
sajada we buy. Then, off duty,
discretely steps out and taking a rod
casts for what he might discover
in rolling turquoise brightness.

In darkness, I see unknown mountains,
enveloped with evergreens, curl
toward seven bare-stone summits
each wrapped in unwarpable
brilliance. You, standing close by,
recite Arabic - *Ya Siin.*

Slow that cosmic prayer moulds
the shore-rocks of our grief and love.

*

Love's Embrace

Farhana Shaikh

I am but *Saif* in your arms,
Proving myself a fool.
Graces I may have been born with
But for you
I will succumb to humble pleasures;
No longer a prince.
I would die a pauper,
For princes are but poor
In the eyes of their beloved
Princesses.
Your beauty is the sweetest rose,
Your father the thorns that pierce me.
I wish to touch thee
Once - promise me,
Be not blinded by the invisible,
It is I who truly loves you,
Not the evil eye,
The Unseen.
Come to me where rivers flow free;
Take my hand then we can sing and dance
To a merry tune,
A love song;
Green eyes can look on
And be tortured.
Come, meet with me just once
And I shall never ask of anything more
Or less,
Just a kiss,
A single embrace;
A closed net at moonlight.

*

Ghazal Pru Kitching
(for Iftikhar Arif)

Big questions sometimes are answered by the river.
Did we love when we collided by the river?

Is our love made holy, are our friendships blessed and
is our existence sanctified by the river?

Like the salmon rising, fighting against the flow,
I flail, out of depth, in the tide of the river.

Who knows the secrets of a heart, of a passion;
a soul or a mind, when it hides by the river?

Can fate be eluded, must derangement prevail?
And who must decide? You decide; you, the river.

Will indecision, Hamlet-like, destroy, wreck, claim
innocents; Ophelias; brides of the river?

Would it matter, then, Vedra, mighty and vengeful,
if calmly and cleanly we died, by the river?

So The Indus Meets The Kabul
Pru Kitching

and so they meet, I remember, in a straight, milky line
and so the milky line seems to be a permanence
and so this permanence is really just an illusion, like a mirage
and so the Mirage flew high and strong
and, so high and strong, head and heart is what they said I had to be
and so, what they said, I was, amid the wreckage
and so the wreckage stayed for years and years and no-one dug
and so, after ages, someone cared and dug down deep
and, so they found me and all my rage

Eyes   *Khadim Hussain*

My eyes were made to see with.
What if they are deceived?

Whose fault is it?
Who do they blame?

The red roses in the flowerbeds?
The pink blossom of the tree?

My naive heart?
Your devious nature?

There are many other flowers;
None are acceptable.

What are the eyes to do?
What are the eyes to do?

Perfection   *David E. Butler*

Revising a Postcard of Islamic History

Dawn at Alhambra. The swifts flick their wings
and fleet into the air, fanning out
before, as if embarrassed,
shadowing the pencil pine
that stands before the turrets of the *Alcazaba.*

She's nervous, being commissioned again, like the first time, except
it's the instinct to perfection she's ashamed of.
                    Two thousand preparatory negatives...

The photographer sniffs the air;
it is sharp, like evaporated stone.
The morning seems hyperventilated, all the particles
of air, brick, stone, wood, her own skin, startled on waking,
do not quite cohere.
She holds the old postcard up to the fort. It looks the same
despite the renovations, except the swifts now scissoring through the air,
snick black rents in the stone.
                    like unrecorded history...

It's said the musicians of the bath house were blinded
so they could not see the women while they played.
But she doesn't believe it.
                    their laughter's patterned in her blood.

She photographed this scene thirty years before
but now she's learnt the trade: this time the swifts will stay.

*

Afreet   *Bob Beagrie*

On the night for finding your one true love
Your notes soothe devils from work sore bones.

On the day you promise to phone home
No satellite can sky-cast your song.

On the night to experience sensual heaven
Mirrors avoid looking you in the eye.

On a day that's a cert. for a stroke of luck
You refuse to see the wood for the trees.

On the night guaranteed to impress new friends
You slice a finger on the stake in your pocket.

On the best day to build on successes
Your eyes are full of distant stars.

On the best night to chill-out alone, you suspect
Ulterior motives in the crack of the wineglass.

On the day for exchanging promises, a Pepsi
Sponsored cyclone steals the wind from your sails.

On the best night to celebrate in style, you quarter
Your heart over a rational argument.

On the day when it all turns pear-shaped, you unfurl
Translucent wings and ride the updrafts out of town.

*

El Diwan
(The Taste of Arabia)

Bob Beagrie

Hold the manakish of the holy month
Between the parched lips of dawn and dusk

Seek the oasis of spices
In the street of false gods

From a shisha pipe's gleam in the corner
A nomadic coil of rose-smoke asks 'Who are you?'

Among minarets and arabesques
I have forgotten my name

Should I wear a fez, spectacles
Grow the grey moustache of a learned man

Become a bird of paradise
Grooming its plumage before morning song

Am I the caterpillar smoking on a mushroom
Dreaming of an emperor-dreaming of a butterfly

I could be the falcon on the glove
Of the Queen of the desert

Loosen my tether, let me fly
Over the jangling line of the caravanserai

Through the drapes, across a bridge of one hair
Kwiksave's auto-doors yawn bargains-in-trolleys

She has set me circling shared homelands
On the dark wings of a prayer

My Dresses   *Afifa Ematullah*

To be dressed in black,
invisibility,
black of every colour.
Ya Allah, veil me from all eyes.

To be dressed in white,
cleanness and purity,
white of no colour.
Hajj-cloth of my name.

But You dressed me
in the gown of midnight and stars:
a background of deep, deep blue,
with milky way and silver of Laila.

You dressed me in Royal Purple,
a robe of honour.

You dressed me
in flowery meadows of paradise,
dewy, pointillist, shimmering,
rainbow-studded, Jameelah.

You dressed me
in sunlit glancing waters,
flashing, dazzling,
platinum and gold of Nuriyyah.

But the dress I liked most
was the one in which I met my love,
the garb of a humble pilgrim
in which he recognised me,

saw my hidden gentleness,
quiet secret deeps of my soul
and named me:
I think you are Halima.
Oh servant of Yours, Ya Allah,
I so wished to be his Halima,
but I only walked behind him
for a while.

*

My Brother The Heron *Afifa Ematullah*

Hard to speak from a wounded heart
to one girded round with grey stone walls.
Dearest brother, you walk near me on a stony road,
bent with weariness.
I look at the sun and shadow of you –
a reality of gentle beauty you find too hard to carry
in a world of scorn.
Long ago, you hid yourself under a disguise.

Take heart
there is nothing you must do to be free.
Your destiny is written, already complete.
Only do not despair,
but love Him who loves you.

A heron finds it hard to walk easily in this world
but when we fly, my brother,
it is all happiness
from Him who loves us.

My Brother The Owl
Afifa Ematullah

You know heartache.
Your ears hear,
in inner silence,
tumult of longing.

Day surrounds you –
your life, working,
talking, moving, playing,
always reasons to say *No*.

Spread your wings,
my night-flying bird,
and soar
through cascading blue and stars!
~
Time to journey into the unknown,
for you are one of His noble warriors.

Be fearless in the landscape of doom.

You, pure of heart, follow Light,
aflame with love

Mirages of hell will explode before you -

they are illusions.

The Soldier

Rubia Begum MWA

Blessed is he who receives His barakah endlessly
From dusk until dawn seeking His pleasure and mercy;
Paths narrow and constrict countlessly
Yet he still strives, and sure footedly climbs.
Up the steep mountain of struggles he goes
And day by day he gets closer and closer,
And though he's scared he may fall… it never shows.
He knows that with Allah everything lies
And places his trust in Him,
So though his back is breaking and he wants to cry
He cannot bring himself to doubt in the Most High.
To the world he seems a hard hearted soldier
Without any real emotion or fear,
With a cold shoulder, hard heart,
Face marked with a sneer,
Cold eyes that you would never have thought
Could even shed a tear.
He walks alone with the angels as his aid
And though he feels his iman about to fade
He lowers his head and begs and prays
To the Lord of the Worlds; he breaks down in shame.
'I am Yours, Allah, Yours;
Do as you please.
I submit to Your Will and I'll beg and I'll plead,
Don't throw me in the fire,
Just spare me please...'

He rises once more and looks ahead,
His mountain of struggles diminished to a heap,
His heart alive, awoken from its sleep -
What you sow, you shall surely reap.

You Could Be...under siege

Zayneb Khan MWA

4th January 2009

You could be London, Madrid, New York, under siege,
You could be my teacher, my soldier, my friend, under siege,
You could be my school, my hospital, my church, under siege,
You could be my tear, my pain, my blood, under siege,
You could be my water, my heat, my bread, under siege,
You could be my shelter, my livelihood, my liberty, under siege,
You could be my innocence, my perception, my reflection, under siege,

> You could be Gaza,
> a place too far for me to see.
> Perhaps you are Gaza
> but your cries are too distant for me.
> You are Gaza
> but those in power have dehumanized you
> so that your suffering does not penetrate me.

Sincere Love
Zayneb Khan MWA

Before you claim to be in love know that
True love is sincerity, not manipulation,
True love is to sacrifice, not to give advice,
True love is to accept, not influence,
True love is to listen attentively before speaking,
True love is to grow and blossom each day together,
True love is to see gifts from The Divine behind layers of sins and regrets,
True love is to be humble, not whine in self arrogance.
True love is to be loved by The Divine through His Creation.

Chateau Chinon, France, November 2007

Flight   *Chris Firth MWA*

In sleep
I became a bird of clay;
I was yearning
For the sweet breath of dawn.
That was me
Singing like an upstart jay
Alone out there
In the apple tree.

My life
Had been lived inside a glass jar
Until You came
Throwing me from a distance.
There was no sky
For me to fly in
Until You came,
Guiding from that certainty
Of the bright star.

Slowly, You hooked on
And bound me;
You lured me on strings
To the temple door.
Gently, You removed my hood
And unwound me
Through doorways
Filled with blue shadow.

'Let go of everything,' You sang,
Or maybe, 'Hold on to nothing.'
It is never easy to translate
The precise wording of dreams.

'Let go of everything,' You sang
'Hold onto nothing.'
Let your head go.
Let everything go.

The Winding Way

Chris Firth MWA

When I searched for You
All I found was shadow
Shifting around my feet;
You were not even gossamer
When I needed concrete.

When I rushed to You
You moved further away
As if playing a game;
You stood in the distance
Teasing out my name.

I took the winding path
Through scrubland wilderness
And You were always elsewhere,
High up in the mountains
Or down in a city square.

When I hid from myself
I found You'd made a home
In the bolt-hole of my heart;
You'd led me on this winding way
Right here to the start.

There is no point in running now –
You are always too fast,
Just ahead of the wind.

There is no point in running now –
We always arrive
Just when we would have
Anyhow.

From 'The Nightingale's Song'

Rumi

"When the rose is gone and the garden faded
You will no longer hear the nightingale's song.
The Beloved is all; the lover just a veil.
The Beloved is living; the lover a dead thing."

Glossary:

These notes have mainly been made where requested by the writers, although some have been made for the sake of clarity and to avoid misunderstandings.

'The Springtime of Lovers' by Rumi. There is always a great deal of scholarly debate about the translation of Rumi's poetry, and obviously nuances of meaning and sound are lost in translation. In some versions of this poem you will see 'a garden' rather than 'Paradise', and 'a diamond' rather than 'a ruby'.

'Afreet' - This poem is from Bob Beagrie's collection *'Hugin & Muninn' (Biscuit Publishing 2002). Afreet* is an accepted variant of *Ifreet* , which are jenii/jinn – good or evil spirits (ie genie).

apsaras - nymphs in Indian Hindu mythology; as with another ghazal in the collection, this one has a Hindu rather than Muslim root.

Alcazaba - the fortified keep at Alhambra Palace, Granada, Spain.

Allah Kareem – God is generous. Also seen as *Karim.* Rooted in Al-Karim, The Generous – one of the 99 Beautiful Names of Allah.

Ayat - a verse of the Qur'an.

As Salaam u Alaikum – 'Peace be with you' – the traditional Islamic greeting.

Awliyah – Saints, the friends of god.

Barakah/baraka - blessings or grace.

Dhikr/zikr - 'Remembrance' – referring to reciting prayers, blessings on the Holy Prophet or reciting/calling the Beautiful Names of Allah.

dum dum tak - the drum beat that forms the basis of Arabian,/Nubian folk music.

Eid Mubarak - congratulations on Eid, traditional greeting given on Eid.

Eid - 'recurring happiness'. It is a day of celebration for Muslims, occurring twice a year, once in the month of Hajj (pilgrimage), and also at the end of Ramadan (the month of fasting), on the first day of the following month.

Hajj cloth - the two lengths of unseamed white cotton fabric that men wear on the pilgrimage (The Hajj) to Makkah and Medinah Munawara.

Haraam – forbidden

Huri/houri – the beautiful maidens and young men of Paradise.

Iman - faith.

Ishtiyaaq - Love.

Jummah - Friday prayers.

Jannatul Firdous/Jennet al Firdaus - the highest level of Paradise. Also the brand name of a popular attar (perfume) traditionally used by men for Eid and Friday prayers.

Kamiz - traditional long shirt worn by both men or women over shalwa, baggy trousers.

Kauthar - a river in Paradise, the spiritual metaphor of a river.

Kurtas – shirt.

Laila/Leila - woman's name meaning *Night of Midnight and Stars.*
Jameelah - woman's name meaning *Beautiful.*
Nuriyyah - woman's name meaning *Light.*
Halima - woman's name, meaning *Gentle One.*
These are left together as all occur in Afifa's poem 'My Dresses', and some in one or two other poems in the collection.

Maqam - tomb or site marking the appearance of a holy person.
The mosque was built on a low rocky seashore.
When Greek Cypriots ruled the area the mosque
was reduced to a household residence; now
it stands restored to a maqam, or sacred site.

Maghrib – Maghrib prayer is one of the 5 compulsory Islamic prayers, prayed after sunset. Asif   Firfirey explains: *this is a poem I wrote recently, about something that genuinely happened when some friends and I went to a kramat (dargah/shrine) on the slopes of the 12 Apostles mountains in Cape Town, South Africa.*

minbar – accepted variant of mimbar – a stepped platform or pulpit in mosques from which prayers, speeches and religious guidance are given.

noor - a spiritual light emitted from the face, person or inner object.

Qiyamah - Judgement. *(Yaum al Qiyama* - Day of Judgement*).*

Saffa - a pure clarity.

Sajada - prayer carpet.

Saif – the poem *'Love's Embrace'* is inspired by a legend of the River Saif, located in North Pakistan, where there is also a beautiful lake. Legend has it that the Crown Prince of Persia heard about the beauty of the fairy Princess, Badar Jamal, the daughter of the King of Caucasus. They met and fell in love. The prince, after many hardships, succeeded in winning the heart of Badar Jamal. The Jinn guard of the Queen of Parbat became jealous of their love and one day breached the bank of the lake to drown them. The lovers escaped and found shelter in a nearby cave. The lake has since become a rendezvous where lovers meet to contemplate matters of heart and their futures together.

shaved head - the poem 'Bedtime Story' refers to the Muslim belief that the signs of end of the world are everywhere, and in particular refers to the belief that it is *haraam* (forbidden) for a Muslim woman to shave her head.

Surah - a 'chapter' of the Qur'an.

Surya - the Hindu Sun-god. *Editor's note*: It is appreciated that this poem is based on Hindu rather than Islamic traditions, at least in content. *'A rug is made of many strands.'*

Tabla - a type of hand drum.

Ya Siin - the 36th 'chapter' of the Qur'an, generally recited for the dying and those already passed away.

Zanana - The women's' quarters.

Biographies of the poets

Jalaluddin RUMI, 1207 -73, was born in Balkh in Afghanistan. A great Islamic scholar and Teacher, he gave up everything to become the disciple of the Darvish, Shamsi Tabriz. In 2008 Rumi was the 'best selling' poet in Europe and the USA. A Muslim, sufi, scholar, teacher, family man, Jalaluddin Rumi was also the founder of the Mevlevi Sufi Order.

Sascha Akhtar lives in London and is originally from Pakistan. She works as journalist and Literary Promoter. Her book *The Grimoire of Grimalkin* was published by Salt publishing in November 2007. Sascha states that: *with the publication of my book by SALT, the world's largest independent literary publisher, I am the first Pakistani woman writing in English to be published in the Western avant-garde tradition.* www.myspace.com/saschaakhtar.

Shameam Akhtar lives in Bradford. She was the winner of the 2008 Muslim Writers' Award for poetry, and was at least short-listed in 2009. Please view the Muslim Writers' Awards website for more information on Shameam and the Muslim Writers' Awards. www.muslimwritersawards.co.uk

Bob Beagrie lives in Middlesbrough. He is a Senior Lecturer in Creative Writing at The University of Teesside. Publications include: *Gothic Horror* (Mudfog 1996), *Masque: The Art of the Vampyre* (Mudfog 2000), *Huginn & Munnin* (Biscuit 2002), *Endeavour: Newfound Notes* (Biscuit 2004), *The Isle of St Hild* (Hartlepool Borough Council 2004), *Perkele* a collaborative bi-lingual pamphlet in English and Finnish, written with Kalle Niinikangas and *Yoik*, (Cinnamon Press 2008). Bob's next collection, *The Seer Sung Husband*, is due out in 2010 from Smokestack Books.

David C. Byrne lives in Manchester. He is a teacher of ESOL to 16-18 year old refugee / asylum seekers. He has been teaching for about ten years and a lot of what he does affects his life and how he views it. He completed an MA in Creative Writing, is involved in performance poetry and as a writer he works in cross-media projects such as film and ceramics. David comments: *I believe very much in the philosophy if you want to then you can do, but you must always try*.

Dr. Debjani Chatterjee, MBE, lives in Sheffield. She is a writer and storyteller with over 50 published books, including *Words Spit and Splinter*, *Namaskar: New and Selected Poems* and *Masala*. Debjani is a Royal Literary Fund Fellow, whose most recent book is *Words Spit and Splinter* (Redbeck Press).

Brian D'Arcy lives in Sheffield. He is a retired Lecturer in Systems. He has two published poetry collections *Tha Shein Ukrosh: Indeed the Hunger* (Bellasis Press) and *Footsteps in the Dust* (Sixties Press). Brian is an Anglo-Irish poet, children's writer and member of the Mini Mushaira writers' group.

Afifa Ematullah lives in Market Rasen, Lincolnshire. For 30 years a disciple of Maulana Sheikh Muhammad Nazim Adil al Haqqani, world leader of the Naqshabandi Sufi Order, she is primarily an artist. The three poems here are from her first collection of poems *'RETURN - Sufi* Poems & Art' was published last year by Dream Catcher Books. Her work has appeared in *Dream Catcher Magazine* and *Tadeeb International*. Her poems have also been selected for inclusion in the anthology, *The Mantle Adorned*, edited by Abdul Hakim Murad, Quilliam Press. Afifa's work can be viewed at www.piscaweb.google.co.uk/islamicart1

Asif Firfirey lives in Scarborough. He is a husband, father to two, teacher/student and poet/word-tamer. He recently won first prize in the North Yorkshire Poetry Competition. Asif had some of his work published in *Al Huda* magazine in South Africa. In his spare time, he works as a General Practitioner and is the Lifeboat Medical Advisor for his local RNLI lifeboat station. Asif states: *I have far to many ideas and far too little time!*

Chris Firth lives in Whitby, Yorkshire. He teaches, writes and edits. He has several books of fiction and poetry published, including Yorkshire Book of The Year, *'North Yorkshire One Nine Nine'*, Shutter Books. Chris comments: *'While working on this book I came across the work of an astounding Iranian poet whose words made my hair stand on end and tears fill my eyes. I refer to Forugh Farrokhzad, who died aged 32.'*

Ustaz Fitrah was born in Port Suakin, on the Red Sea Coast of The Republic of Sudan. He is currently living in Bristol, working as a landscape gardener. He is a poet, musician and song-writer, and he says that his words here are song lyrics rather than poems. His first collection of lyrics and poetry, *'Black Light Sama'*, is to be published by Shutter Books in 2009.

Ameena Zameer Hanif lives in Birmingham. She is a Primary School Teacher. Publications of her work are in Anchor Books, The International Library of Poetry, and more recently online at www.publishingbirmingham.com. Ameena states: *On the 28th March 2007, I was presented with the first annual Muslim Writers Award for Poetry. I appeared on 'Your Event' on the Islam Channel and was interviewed on 'Saturday Nite Live' with other award winners. In 2008, I was short-listed for the non-fiction award.*

Khadim Hussain has lived in Middlesbrough since 1975. His book *'Going for a Curry? A Social and Culinary History'* documents the settlement, development and impact of the 'Indian' population in Middlesbrough. He recently completed an MA in Creative Writing at the University of Teesside, and has since started writing plays and poetry. His poetry collection *'Walayat Deko'* was published by Mudfog in 2008.

Shelina Zahra Janmohamed lives in London. She is an author, blogger and Marketing Manager. She is author of the book *'Love in a Headscarf'*, a humorous memoir of growing up as a Muslim woman looking for love. Shelina has her own blog at www.spirit21.co.uk, and comments regularly in the media including The Guardian, BBC and EMEL magazine.

Ahmed Khan lives in Birmingham. These poems are his first published work. These poems are dedicated to the awaliyah (friends of God).
Ahmed is currently undertaking master classes in playwrighting with Ola Onimashiwun at the Royal Court Theatre in London. He has scripted a full length stage play.

Sitara Khan lives in Leeds. She trained as a teacher, and has held a number of management positions in Education. She is the author of *'A Glimpse through Purdah – Asian Women, the Myth and the Reality'*, Trentham Books in 1999. Her poems and short stories have appeared in a range of publications in the UK and internationally. A collection of her poetry is due to be published by Flux Gallery Press.

Aysha Khanom lives in Rawtenstall. She is currently a student. She has been published in *Al Ameen Newspaper,* Canada, *Muslim Writer Awards Magazine*, and is a contributing writer at suhaibwebb.com. Aysha comments: *Strive to be amongst those who spread justice in the world with their hands and speech.*

Pru Kitching lives in Weardale in the North Pennines. Her first poetry pamphlet, *All Aboard the Moving Staircase,* was published in 2004 by Vane Women Press. Her second poetry pamphlet, *The Krakow Egg*, was published 2009 by Arrowhead Poetry. Pru has just won a Northern Promise Award from New Writing North. The two poems in this anthology are also published in *The Krakow Egg.*

Abu Madjnuun lives in Slough. He is a bridge and highways engineer. This is his first published poem. He is writing a collection of modern love poetry. Madjnuun comments: *I am fascinated by the concept of love and the cultural madness that surrounds it.*

Nafees Mahmud lives in Glasgow, Scotland. This is his first published poem. He is currently co-directing a self written play *'On the Couch'*.

Sufi Punk lives in Birmingham and is an Artistic Director. The poem here is taken from the Ulfah Arts Production called *Danger! Gulaam Fatima*.
Sufi Punk believes in the shared attitude that can create two different extremes.

Romana Qureshi lives in Birmingham. She is a Public Relations Officer and Photographer.

This is her first published work and was Inspired during a spiritual retreat hearing a teacher's and a young girl's stories of their fathers.

Romana comments: *At moments when unable to speak of what is deeply felt, the ink becomes a companion, beholding emotions and beauty forever.*

Farhana Shaikh lives in Leicester. She is the founding Editor of *The Asian Writer* She has had one previously published poem - 'My Teacher' - in an anthology when she was 11.

Farhana was inspired to become a writer at a young age after meeting Alan Ahlberg.

Adam Strickson lives in Wellhouse, Golcar, near Huddersfield. He is a freelance poet, scriptwriter and Teaching Fellow in Creative Writing at the University of Leeds. His publications include *'An Indian Rug Surprised by Snow'*, Wrecking Ball Press and he is one of six writers featured in *'Interland: Six Steps Underwater'*, Smith/Doorstop Books. Adam has worked on drama and writing projects with Muslim communities in Yorkshire, the North West and Bangladesh for twenty years, with enduring friendships and fruitful collaborations made along the way.

Paul Sutherland is an award winning Canadian-British poet who arrived in the UK in 1973. He is founding editor of *Dream Catcher,* a distinguished international literary journal. He has had six collections of poetry published and has edited several others. *Seven Earth Odes*, (Endpapers Press, 2004) won critical praise in the UK, US and Canada. Paul is seeking a publisher for his next collection *Journeyings*. Paul is a sufi muslim, and is now also known and writing as Abdul Wadud.

Mariette Thorburn lives in Halifax, West Yorkshire. She is a poet and musician. A collection of her poetry with the working title of *'Occasional China'* is to be published by Comma Press, and she is currently working on an illustrated story for children about a beautiful but dead dog. Mariette, a student of Appalachian dance, has a weekly radio slot on Phoenix Radio FM, Halifax.

Rubia Begum, *MWA*; **Zayneb Khan** *MWA*; **Nooruddean Choudry**, *MWA*.

These 3 writers were short-listed for the 2009 Muslim Writers' Award for poetry and no biographical information was available at time of going to print. Please view the Muslim Writers' Awards website for information on these writers and the Muslim Writers' Awards: www.muslimwritersawards.co.uk

Other publications by Shutter Books and electraglade:

Whitby One Nine Nine – Richard Jemison (photography) and Chris Firth (poetry)
'This book is life enhancing!' – Lord Crathorne.
Introduction by Lord Crathorne, Lord Lieutenant of North Yorkshire to HM Queen Elizabeth II.
Shutter Books ISBN 0-9551307-0-0

North Yorkshire One Nine Nine – Richard Jemison, Nigel Whitfield (photography) and Chris Firth (poetry) – with contributions from poets across the UK.
Yorkshire Book Of The Year (non-fiction) 2007-8. Supported by Arts Council England.
Introduction by Rt. Hon. William Hague MP.
'There is so much to treasure in this book. Anyone who loves this county in which we live will find it a joy.' Stephen Lewis – York Evening Press.
Shutter Books ISBN ISBN 0-9551307-3-5

Teesway One Nine Nine - Richard Jemison, Nigel Whitfield (photography) and Chris Firth (poetry) – with contributions from poets across North East of England.
'Teesway One Nine Nine is a beautiful chronicle of lives, landscapes and hidden visual depths in the North East of England. Stunning and original!'
Introduction by Kathryn Armstrong, editor of North East Exclusive Magazine.
Shutter Books ISBN 978-0-9551307-5-5

North Yorkshire Naturally – Richard Jemison and Nigel Whitfield (inspirational photography).
Shutter Books ISBN 0-9551307-1-9

Forthcoming:

The Harrogate Book – Richard Jemison, Nigel Whitfield (photography)
and various contributors (factual text).
Shutterer Books ISBN 978-0-9551307-6-2

Black Light Sama – Ustaz Fitrah
Spiritual song lyrics and love poetry of simplicity, depth and great beauty.
electraglade/Shutter Books ISBN 978-0-9551307-9-3

Orders and further information:
 www.jemisonphotographer.co.uk
samaghazal@hotmail.co.uk
electraglade@aol.com